Peoples
of the
Plains

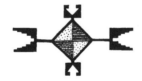

Thomas E. Mails

Illustrations by the Author

COUNCIL OAK BOOKS

Quotes are taken from the following books:

Brown, Joseph Epes. *The Sacred Pipe,* University of Oklahoma Press, Norman, 1953.

Catlin, George. *Letters and Notes on the Manners, Customs, and Condition of the North American Indians,* Vols. 1 and 2. Ross and Haines, Inc., Minneapolis, 1965.

DeVoto, Bernard. *Across the Wide Missouri.* Houghton-Mifflin Co., Boston; Riverside Press, Cambridge, 1947.

Dodge, Colonel Richard Irving. *The Plains of the Great West.* Archer House, Inc., New York, 1959.

Dorsey, George A. *Traditions of the Skidi Pawnee.* Houghton, Mifflin and Company, Boston and New York, 1904.

Ewers, John C. *Artists of the Old West.* Doubleday & Company, Inc., Garden City, New York, 1965.

Linderman, Frank B. *Plenty Coups, Chief of the Crows.* University of Nebraska Press, Lincoln, 1962.

Lowie, Robert H. *The Crow Indians.* Holt, Rinehart & Winston, New York, 1956.

McClintock, Walter. *The Old North Trail, Life, Legends and Religion of the Blackfeet Indians.* University of Nebraska Press, Lincoln, 1968.

Wilson, E.N. *The White Indian Boy* (Pioneer Life Series). World Book Co., Yonkers-on-Hudson, New York, 1922.

Council Oak Books, Tulsa, OK 74120

01 00 99 98 97   5 4 3 2 1

Library of Congress cataloging-in-publication data

Mails, Thomas E.
    Peoples of the Plains / Thomas E. Mails; illustrations by the author.
        p. cm. — (The Library of Native Peoples)
    "Originally published in a slightly different version in Mystic Warriors of the Plains. c1972, c1991"—CIP galley.
    ISBN 1-57178-046-7 (alk. paper)
    1. Indians of North America—Great Plains.   I. Mails, Thomas E.
    Mystic Warriors of the Plains.   II. Title.   III. Series.
    E78.G73M343   1997
    978' .00497—dc21   97-12698
                                                CIP

Edited and Designed by Tony Meisel, AM Publishing Services
Printed in the United States of America
ISBN 1-57178-046-7

Contents

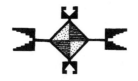

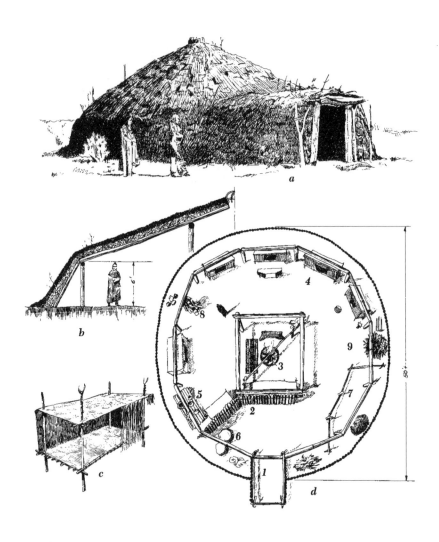

Stationary tribe earth lodge. *a*, exterior of Pawnee lodge. *b*, section through lodge showing post framework covered with thick layer of brush and sod. *c*, typical bed. *d*, Hidatsa earth lodge floor plan: *1*, entrance; *2*, screen wall; *3*, fireplace; *4*, beds; *5*, food platform; *6*, bull boats; *7*, corral; *8*, shrine; *9*, firewood.

Manner of Daily Life

While the ancient Plains population was not, by modern comparisons, huge, even the individual tribes were much too large to travel and to pursue their way of life as a single group. So for many reasons, not the least of which was good sense, they subdivided into small bands which were made up of unrelated families, or into clans consisting of persons related by marriage, and went their independent ways within prescribed boundaries. Usually they assembled upon notice for one or two grand tribal buffalo hunts, fall and spring, and once during the early summer for the annual games and Sun Dance. They also gathered on rare occasions for massive tribal defense. The one exception to this dispersal of the tribes was the few earth lodge groups who lived together as a single unit most of the time.

Two types of dwellings were used by the Plains tribes: the better-known ingenious buffalo hide tipi, and the more permanent earth or bark lodges of a few small and generally stationary agricultural groups such as the Arikara, Mandan, Omaha, and Pawnee. Even then, all tribes employed the tipi while on the move. The buffalo hide tipi and all of its contents easily deserve a place among the world's leading examples of classic mobile design. Averaging fourteen feet in diameter and large enough to house an average family of five to eight persons, it could be set up by a woman in less than fifteen minutes and taken down in three. The homes and furnishings of an entire camp could be packed upon horse or dog-drawn travois and on the move in twenty minutes. The tipi, assisted by only a brush fence, carried its occupants through the worst winters using minimum fuel, and with rolled-up sides became a vented summer umbrella. During the day its translucent walls admitted a pleasant light, and at night each dwelling transformed itself into a giant candle to illuminate the camp. It required no painting, save decoration, and was repaired simply by patching.

Since most Plains Indians moved with the buffalo during all but the winter months, their camps advanced within their own territory every few days, moving ten or fifteen miles each time. In so doing, some important side functions were served. The elements disposed of the sanitation problems after they moved on, and the migration itself was a source of constat excitement and adventure.

Generally speaking, a tribe hunted within its own domain, and the territorial boundaries became the only common hunting grounds; a situation which, however, often led to some sudden and spirited engagements between tribes. Ordinarily small war and raiding parties were the only groups to invade the heartland of the dangerous neighboring areas—the exception being times when hunger drove entire tribal

Plains Indian buffalo-hide tipi. *a,* side view. *b,* front view. *c,* tipi pattern. *d,* quilled tipi ornament. *e,* hide door cover. *f,* Sioux floor plan: *1,* entrance; *2,* fireplace; *3,* altar; *4,* beds; *5,* firewood; *6,* poles.

divisions to it.

By and large the Plains Indians lived on buffalo meat. The earth lodge tribes grew corn, squash, beans, and a few other vegetables, but the rest gathered only small seasonal amounts of wild berries, chokecherries, turnips, and later a few other items obtained in intertribal or White trade, to add to their diet. On the somewhat rare mountain trips, antelope, elk, and deer meat was obtained, but it never replaced the buffalo. Mountain sheep skins were used for clothing, and while I've not found evidence of the Native Americans' eating the meat, they probably did. Most tribes did not care for fish, although some tribes, such as the stationary Mandans who lived on the Missouri, Heart, and Knife rivers, and the Eastern Rockies Utes and Shoshones—who made infrequent forays onto the western edge of the Plains for buffalo—did catch and eat them. Of course, Native Americans ate whatever they could catch when they were hungry enough. Now and then, even dogs and horses were killed to provide their meals.

The desired village sites for the nomadic tribes were those which offered a good water supply, ample wood, grazing and forage for horses, protection from wind, and security from enemies. Level, wooded bottom lands cradled by bluffs or ridges were generally sought. At the tribal assemblies, however, they camped on the high flatter ground, pitching their tipis in a great circle with the main entrance to the east. The usual village plan was an informal assemblage of lodges, with the location of each tipi determined by family relationship, position in the previous

Tipi details. *a*, sides rolled up for summer ventilation. *b*, section through tipi wall showing outside cover and liner. *c*, buffalo-hide liner.

village site, and geographical configuration. Relatives tended to live near one another, but when a new household was set up the owners were at liberty to place their lodges wherever they wished.

To select the best campground, even for a night on the Plains, required instinct, excellent judgment, and a knowledge of all the possibilities facing the camper. There were numerous questions involving the comfort and safety of the party to be decided by the camp leader as camping time arrived, and the fact that a Native American chief could constantly select a camp capable of supplying their varied wants testifies to a high degree of competence. He had to take into account the clan's own comfort and that of its stock. And, he must consider all of the dangers to which they might be exposed, either from human enemies or from the elements. A hunting party would choose a different site than a war party, and each in making its selection had to relate its objects and intentions to all the surrounding possibilities.

Colonel Richard Irving Dodge once followed a predatory party of Comanches for more than thirty days, and the camp in which he finally surprised them was the only site in all that time that could have been approached without discovery. (Dodge, *Thirty-Three Years Among Our Wild Indians,* p. 240)

Except in winter, the location of a camp indicated something of its occupants. A camp near water and away from all timber was probably Sioux, who had a deep respect for ambush; a camp on open prairie, but near timber, would be Cheyenne or Arapaho; a camp situated among open timber, Kiowas or Comanches; while smoke issuing from the cover of a dense thicket would indicate Osages, Omahas, or Pawnees.

During the spring months, tipis were repaired or renewed from new hides which had been collected during the fall and winter. Leggings and moccasins were made from the "smoked tops," and the smoking of hides for all uses began with the arrival of warm weather. The society clubs put on their mesmerizing dances, and the vital vision-seeking rites continued from late spring until the snow fell in October or November. In May the bands moved from their winter settlements to higher ground. This movement was traditional and not entirely the result of necessity. If food supplies were low, a buffalo hunt was planned to coincide with this migration. During the early summer months, individual family hunts were carried out, with men and boys hunting game for their household on a regular basis. When not occupied with this, they constructed and repaired their weapons. Meanwhile, the women were busy gathering early roots and berries. Hide painting was done while the weather was bright and warm, and at this time sweet-smelling leaves were gathered and preserved, especially during the Moon of the Ripe June Berries. Limited tribal hunts were organized whenever a herd of buffalo was sighted.

The major part of the summer was given over to ceremonial affairs. It was the master season of celebration; there was vision-seeking and cult performances, there were society elections and even such exotic occasions as female virtue feasts, and the stupendous Sun Dance served as the monumental climax of the ceremonial season.

As the festival season ended for most tribes, a fall hunt was immediately organized. In some tribes, however, there was no formalized communal hunt as such, rather the great camp circle broke up, and the individual bands set out to hunt on their own.

Autumn was an equally busy time of year. Women gathered their auxiliary foods and dried buffalo meat in preparation for the approaching winter. Men hunted intensely so that the supply of meat would be

Grazing buffalo.

adequate, and when the season drew to a close underground caches were prepared as winter insurance. Wood was gathered wherever possible to provide fuel for the winter.

In addition to the activities described thus far, male war and raiding parties were conducted during all but the worst weeks of the winter. Small groups left their base camp at irregular intervals, often being away for weeks, and always had to catch up with the main migrating group upon their return.

Taking their guidance from what they saw during the reservation period, some people have decided that the Plains Indians sat around and did nothing most of the time. Yet this is a superficial judgment made when they could no longer move freely about and their befouled camps were no longer cleaned by nature. On the contrary, before this time they were a very industrious people, and their magnificent productivity and accomplishments make this abundantly clear.

In amplification of this truth, Maximilian visited a Blackfoot Indian camp, and returned with the following vivid description of its activity:

> Maximilian watched the preparation of furs, the making of pemmican, the constant tailoring and dressmaking of the women. The handicrafts of the polished-stone age were going on all around him and he filled a lot of notebooks. The Blackfeet were not so good at them as some of the Plains tribes and had to keep interrupting their warfare so that they could trade, especially with their inveterate enemies the Crows, for bonnets and decorated robes and clothes and weapons and parfleches and utensils. Their ceremonies were without end; dances to bring

the buffalo or to propitiate some supernatural who had indicated his displeasure, seasonal observances that had to be made at the appointed time, private magic or goopher dust that required the cooperation of neighbors, fraternity rites, lodge meetings, supplications for aphrodisiacs, commemoration of the heroes. Town criers were always summoning emergency assemblies to meet special situations and the normal death rate was always adding mourning shrieks to the bedlam and amputated fingers to the general bloodiness. Someone was always yelling and clattering rattles to scare diseases out of the sick. The beauty of Indian music, whether vocal or instrumental, is somewhat esoteric to such white men as do not live in Santa Fe and Maximilian's ears suffered from an energetic, lethally monotonous caterwauling that nothing could shut off. Day or night there was no escape from the drums, the thump of moccasined feet, and the singing that was just "hi-ya" in Indian scales. Observation of other tribes had made Maximilian a sophisticate; the jugglery of the Blackfoot medicine men, he found, was not up to Broadway.

DeVoto, *Across the Wide Missouri*, p. 139

Even while the camp was moving, the tumultuous picture changed very little, as the following description of the Shoshones on their way to a celebration indicates:

About two hundred and fifty braves on their best horses—and they bought good ones from the Nez Percés—rode in full dress ahead of the village. Stately chiefs, caracoling horses, medicine men juggling as they rode, deep-voiced chants, warwhoops, muskets firing, arrows skittering across the plain. Sometimes a squad of young braves break into a gallop, angling away from the column in pursuit of imaginary Sioux, hanging by their heels on the far side of their horses, shooting arrows under their necks. Other performers do all the tricks that are still called

Horse and Dog travois. *a*, horse travois. *b*, Blackfeet women using travois. *c*, method of transporting incapacitated person. *d*, Cheyenne willow basket to protect or cover children on travois. *e*, dog travois. *f*, dog with travois—Blackfeet.

Cossack. Others leap to the ground and take imaginary scalps, then ride on singing the scalp song. Everything is orderly again when the procession nears the Company camp—columns of files, lances and painted war shields at salute, dignity swelling the noble chests and making the noble faces solemn ... And behind them the Snake village is strung out for well over a mile, dust from the scraping travois, from the horse herd which the boys are driving, from the interweaving horses of the women. Old men and women ride the travois atop the piled tipis and parfleches; so do young children. Stolid babies swathed to the chin in cradles stare out from their mothers' backs. The ladies who have to manage all this are shrill and profane. There is an incessant brawling of excited dogs. Reaching the river and its cottonwoods, the village breaks up into its components. Even noisier now, the women help one another put up the tipis. The horses are watered and herded across the plain.

DeVoto, p. 322-23

Since the Shoshones were poor in comparison to the huge and prosperous tribes, one can easily imagine what the Sioux, Blackfoot, Assiniboine, and Comanche parades or migrations were like.

When the first heavy snows were about to fall, the bands and clans gathered at a predetermined place to decide upon the permanent winter camp sites. Once selected and occupied, these locations were used until March or April.

The winter camp was regarded by the Native American as his true home. The intensity of war, hunting, and constant movement slacked off, and he settled down to a period of preparation for the more vigorous seasons to come.

When a winter site was selected, the entire tribe went to it *en masse,*

Camp leader and assistants selecting camp site.

but there was no attempt at order in the location of the lodges. The followers of a given chief might be scattered for miles, each taking advantage of the sheltered nooks formed by thickets or bluffs. The great questions facing each Native American were shelter, convenience, and feed for the ponies, though the desire to keep as near to each other as possible was obviously served.

A winter camp might occupy a mile one winter, and the next would extend as much as six miles along a stream. Sometimes several friendly tribes occupied the same stream and made an immense camp.

Native Americans at relative peace and with plenty of food found the winter camp a place of constant enjoyment. The prospect of rest, with its home life and pleasures, came like a soothing balm to all.

The aged warriors spent their daylight hours in gambling, their long winter evenings in endless repetitions of stories of their noble performances in days gone by, and their nights in restful sleep. It is said by those who shared these sessions that the Native Americans were as exciting storytellers as ever lived. They knew how to capture the listener's attention, and how to fix a story in his mind.

There was even another, and perhaps more important, kind of storytelling going on. As the Native Americans had no written records, the maintenance of their historical accounts depended altogether on oral tradition. Therefore, each tribe had its historians who considered it their sacred duty to instruct selected young men carefully in the traditions of the nation, just as their own teachers had taught them. The pupils would gather in the lodges, and the old men would repeat in words and actions the captivating tales again and again, until at last the hearers had committed them to memory. In this way the sacred stories, elaborate rituals, and all the tribal history were handed down. The old men who were most learned in this ancient lore took an immense pride in their knowledge, and had a consuming desire to transmit it in the

Native American village.

precise form in which they received it. If, among his descendants, one found a boy who manifested a special interest in the stories, or showed a marked capacity for remembering them, he redoubled his efforts to perfect him in this learning. To some he would present certain old stories as gifts, and these, thereafter, might not be related by another until the recipient passed them on.

The women enjoyed the winter too, for the hectic taking down and putting up of the tipis ended, as did the packing and unpacking of bags and ponies. The stormbound days and longer evenings of winter made it the ideal time for the women to manufacture and repair clothing and they were forever busy with their rolled skins and awls. Sinew, especially that taken from alongside the buffalo's back and leg bones, was the Native American's thread. Splitting it for size was a task requiring great skill. Each of those taken from the different parts of the body had its own properties which made it best for specific uses. The women had been diligently trained in sewing from early childhood, and produced, as any museum reveals, some of the finest artwork in the world. Beads, porcupine quills, bird quills, grasses, paints, ermine tails, fringes of other fine furs, small animal and bird bones, bars of metal, bells, braided hair, and fleeces appeared as if by magic from the hide container which the seamstress had added to and repacked at every move throughout the year.

The clothes maker worked in traditions of art and craft that were old and rigid. As with the man's duties, religious rituals to guarantee

Nez Percé woman making pemmican.

quality were a part of every task; so too were certain social obligations to older women who had either taught them their skills, or sold their right to use them. A specialized item such as a chief's gift, or even some steps in the making of an ordinary item, might be forbidden to any but those who had the right, and these would perform them with the proper accompanying fees and feasts. Generally speaking, any woman at work was a skilled artisan and a happy one. She sang, chattered, made jokes, and evidenced pride in the highest degree.

The Native American woman was not, as is commonly thought, a drudge or slave. White men who lived with the Native Americans, such as Grinnell, Schultz, and McClintock, deride this notion as an erroneous one, and avoid the use of the demeaning title "squaw." Women did do all the hard camp work. They cooked, brought wood and water, dried the meat, dressed the robes, made the clothing, collected the lodge poles, packed the horses, cultivated the ground, and generally performed all the tasks which might be called menial; but no one thought of them as servants in this. On the contrary, their position was respected and their crafts were highly valued. A man's offer to help with the difficult female tasks would always be scorned. He had his place, and the women had theirs. Then too, wives were always consulted on intimate family affairs and often in more general matters. They also shared jointly with their husbands in sacred rituals. A few women were even admitted to the band councils, and gave advice there. Assuredly, the privilege was unusual, and only granted to women who had performed a deed comparable to those of the leading men of the tribe, but it did happen!

A wife did not hesitate to interrupt and correct her husband, and the husband listened with respectful attention, though of course the amount of it depended somewhat upon her proven intelligence. So while their lives were hard, they still found time to contribute, to gossip, and to gamble, and on the whole managed considerable pleasure in life. Seldom did a Native American wife want to trade what she had for the manner of existence she saw among wives in the non-Native American world.

The Native American ladies readily endorsed the idea of polygamous marriages. Battle deaths often left a plurality of husbandless women behind. Then too, the hard labor involved in their chores became easier as it was divided among a number of wives. In most tribes, tradition gave a woman's husband first claim on her younger sisters as his additional wives, and if there were no sisters, the original wife sometimes turned to other families to obtain a second wife for him. In any case she remained number one, there was less work for her to do, and she always had somebody to talk to when her husband was away on his hunting or warring trips.

The faulty attitudes of Whites about Native American women was often revealed by their seeming readiness to misunderstand these wonderful people. For instance, many a White person was dismayed as he saw the Native American wife trudging along behind her husband; she carrying a bulky load on her back, while he carried only his weapons. Yet Native Americans would explain that he was in front of her to

Cheyenne women fleshing buffalo hides.

break the trail in summer and winter, and carried just his weapons so as to be unimpeded and instantly ready to defend her against attack. By this he fulfilled the vows he made to her to do this very thing on their wedding day, and she was pleased that he did, since her life depended on it.

Men could not marry until they had *earned* the right. Among the Crows, this meant they did not marry until they were either twenty-five or had counted coup, that is, touched an enemy during combat with something held in their hand. Plenty Coups, a chief of the Crows, explained that the custom was followed because a man who had counted coup or reached the age of twenty-five was considered to be strong and healthy. He pointed out that "men breed their horses with great care, but often forget themselves in this respect. When a man breaks a traditional law and marries any woman whenever he can, imperfectly formed children are born." (Linderman, *Plenty Coups,* pp. 118, 206) Yet the chief had never heard of a deformed Crow child when he was a young man on the Plains, and while the old ways were still being followed.

In the ancient Crow law governing marriage, no man could wed a woman belonging to the same clan as his own. Children always belonged to the clan of their mother, and the law prevented the possibility of inbreeding, because when they married they had to mate with those of another clan. Occasionally new blood was infused by unions with members of other tribes, so that, the Native Americans say, "the race did not decline." Native Americans were high in their praises of the

Cheyenne men making bows.

law that permitted men to marry under twenty-five only if they had counted coup. The rule made them strive to be strong and brave, and they believed that a man could be neither without good health through physical activity. To show how far they pursued these ideals, even though the law permitted a Crow man who had reached the age of twenty-five years and had not counted coup to take a wife, he could not "paint his woman's face," which was something every real warrior did each morning, so that even this tribal distinction was withheld from both of them, and the incentive to bravery and tribal defense was kept to the fore.

In horse parades and while moving the camp the wife often rode her husband's best war horse and carried his lance and shield, proud to be united with him as one person in all they did together. Many tribes had no formal wedding service, but in some tribal marriage ceremonies, a thumb of each was cut slightly, and the two thumbs tied together. As the blood mingled, the officiant declared they were now as one, just as the blood was one, and they were commanded to live as "one flesh" ever after. Such vows were just as sincere and effective as we intend them to be when they are repeated in marriage ceremonies today.

Morally, the Native Americans did remarkably well at setting commendable standards for a supposedly primitive people, and at times performed better than many of what are considered to be the more civilized nations. In fact, their moral decline during the treaty and reservation period bears an almost direct ratio to the amount of contact occurring between the White and Red races.

Feminine chastity was highly prized, and a suitor would only offer expensive gifts for a virtuous girl. Likewise, certain honored tasks at the sacred ceremonies could be carried out only by a woman of irreproachable purity.

The Pawnees did some wife sharing on a temporary basis, but the practice was not characteristic of the area. Some tribes allowed a husband to disfigure a promiscuous wife. The Blackfeet and Piegans cut off the woman's nose, and thus marked her for life. A prosperous Native American male might, as previously stated, have several wives—sometimes as many as four or five. Yet most marriages by far were monogamous. As for divorce, a marriage could be dissolved without fuss, and often was. But a faithful and industrious woman was seldom cast out.

Returning, however, to the winter season, and concluding our

Assiniboine hunter with hunting dogs.

thoughts regarding it, it brought a special and unending period of excitement of the young. During the day there were new games, dances and feasts, visits and frolics; pleasures of every kind. At night by the flickering fires of the tipis the storytellers prepared, rehearsed, and presented their marvelous recitals. Above all it was the season for love-making, and it was said that "Winter was the time when love rules the camp."

Echoing the conclusions of all who knew them well, Colonel Dodge pointed out the numerous faults of the Native Americans, but also said:

These primitive people are habitually and universally, the happiest people I ever saw. They thoroughly enjoy the present, make no worry over the possibilities of the future, and never

Tipi details. *a,* winter tipi with brush shelter wall. *b,* travois loaded with folded tipi. *c,* winter food caches.

Village herald or "crier," who announced important matters.

cry over spilt milk . . . . The Native American man never broods, and in spite of that dreadful institution, polygamy, and the fact that the wives were mere property, the domestic life of the Native American will bear comparison with that of average civilized communities. The husband as a rule, is kind; ruling, but with no harshness. The wives are generally faithful, obedient, and industrious. The children are spoiled, and a nuisance to all visitors. Among themselves, the members of the family are perfectly easy and unstrained. It is extremely rare that there is any quarreling among the wives. There is no such thing as nervousness in either sex. Everybody in the lodge seems to do just as he or she pleases, and this seems no annoyance to anybody else.

Dodge, p. 248

Few can deny that the life pattern of the Plains Indians included

Sioux warrior playing love flute.

much to recommend it to others. The Native Americans themselves deeply regretted its loss, and hearkened back to it in the most poignant of terms—as did sympathetic Whites who were able to live with them in such a way as to appreciate their manner and intent.

E. N. Wilson, a White boy who lived for two years with the Shoshones, states that his Native American mother "was as good and kind to him as any one could be." When he pleased her by an act or remark, her face would "light up," and sometimes a tear would steal down her brown cheeks. Then she would grab him and hug him "until you could hear his ribs crack." In fact, she did everything she could to make him happy. (Wilson, *The White Indian Boy,* pp. 39-40)

The Native Americans regularly include statements similar to the following in their stories of olden days:

"The weather was cold [as we began our war party trip], but in those days in all kinds of weather men had good times. Cold days were the same to us as warm ones, and we were nearly always happy!"

"At returning home to see the clans gathered, our hearts sang with the thought of visiting friends we had not seen in a long time."

"It was good to live in those days!"

"Those were happy days," the old warrior said softly. "Our bodies were strong and our minds healthy because there was always something for both to do. When the buffalo went away we became a changed people." (Linderman, p. 118)

Clearly, the Plains Indians of the year 1800 were an industrious,

Plenty Coups, great chief of the crows (1850–1932) (adaptation from photograph taken in Washington, D.C., in 1921).

unburdened, moral, sensitive, and contented people. They had evolved a way of life which produced a healthy and productive society—devoid of disabling mental distresses and having no need for drugs and excesses to dull the senses. The very young child was free to play with reckless abandonment, but the rest of the community maintained a careful balance each passing day between industry, pleasure, and religion.

Native American religion has received but the briefest mention thus far, yet only because it was so vital and comprehensive. While religion was participated in fervently by everyone, it remained an individual and personal matter of the greatest portent. In fact, it was the source and center of each Native American's life. This being the case, the treatment of the Plains Indian religion are given a much broader coverage in *Spirits of the Plains* (available as part of the Library of Native Peoples Series). Here the tribal social life and governmental forms will be considered, with exemplary personal attributes and religion being brought in as the capstones of the total picture.

Ermine headdress used in the ceremonies of the Blackfoot Horn Society. Members were believed to have enough supernatural power to cause death, and were greatly respected by the other members of the tribe.

Social Customs

The Plains Indians lived in circumstances which made them constantly aware of the capricious forces of nature, of their vulnerability to attack, and of their responsibilities, yet they loved living, and a sizable portion of their time was given over to social activities and events. A group spirit pervaded every village. People enjoyed eating and talking together, and hospitality was a norm of life. Everyone agreed that for the general good of the community as a whole it was better to give than to receive. The mathematics of such a course recommended itself highly, for while an individual watching out for himself might gain the minor securities self-trust brings, the social plan brought each person the comforting assurance that as he looked out for others, everyone in the village was looking out for him. Therefore, the village had a summary strength; the abilities of each multiplied by the number present, and the tribe as a whole developed a corresponding power.

The social life manifested itself at four levels or strata. First of all, the intimacy of the band and the clan kinship ties afforded numerous opportunities for close fellowship within each family and between

a, Black Eagle, leader of the Blackfoot Kisapa (Hair Parters) Dance. The Kisapa was a social organization composed of young men. *b*, typical society rattles.

families. Communal eating and conversation was a regular thing. Chores were often shared, and there was a constant interchange of gifts. Male heroes received especially warm attention from the immediate family, since the status of anyone was enhanced by his association with an acknowledged leader. Beyond this, personal fellowship carried over into tribal relationships, since friendships were engendered and matured over the years, and the annual tribal encampments afforded grand opportunities to renew cherished relationships of long standing. Native Americans on their way to the great tribal gatherings were usually brimming over with emotion and anticipation, barely able to contain themselves until the reunion took place and anxious to discover what had happened since last they met.

A second stratum of social life took place at the community level, since the entire village shared in an annual cycle of religious events, in the dissemination of all important news and its consequences, in some buffalo hunts, in victory celebrations, in dances, and in the frequent migratory movements. Thus while each person maintained his individuality, he never did so to the point where he considered it more important than his place in the village and tribe. Of course there were occasional frictions which divided people and altered loyalties, but for the most part, a given individual was always a vital part of a greater whole. And so he or she sought constant opportunities to solidify the unit by creative participation in community events.

The third and fourth strata of social life were natural outcomes of the interdependent attitude of the individual in his community. Moving beyond the family level, community activities were played out in a heightened sense at the tribal level. Annual encampments afforded opportunities for council meetings, clothing comparisons, craft displays, trading, huge dances, horse races, gambling, rampant gossiping, games, lovemaking, hero adulation, and the like. Everything common to a family was also the norm for the tribe. And, all in all, it made for a very rich life.

The fourth and highest stratum of social existence will be readily understood by those who are members of present-day clubs or secret societies, since they will appreciate the social and psychological function such organizations serve for the individual, and for the public as a whole. If anything, this was truer still of the Plains Indians, since the societies played a vital and dramatic role in the life of the village and tribe.

Societies were sometimes borrowed from another tribe, but most had their beginning in the vision or dream of the man who thereafter became the founder. The vision would set forth the society's purpose, the number of its members, and at least the rough form of the society's colors, symbols, garb, dances, songs, and rituals. Once the vision was accepted as legitimate by the tribe's elders, other people were invited to join, and the society was born.

Subsequent visions might contain information which helped to enlarge the concept and costume of the club, but its initial purpose seldom changed a great deal. The order of rank in the band was usually

Society equipment. *a*, typical wooden, curved society staff or lance wrapped with otter fur and adorned with ribbons and eagle feathers. This type of staff also identified assistant war party leaders. The warrior also wears the more common version of the short soldier sash, which was about seven feet long. *b*, the neck insertion method of wearing the sash. *c*, the shoulder loop method of wearing the sash. *d*, Crow warrior carrying feathered coup stick. *e*, typical willow coup stick. *f*, Sioux warrior holding leader's flag.

determined by the date of origin of the club, with the most ancient society being accorded the highest rank, and after it the next oldest, etc.

While most societies were made up exclusively of male participants, many of them had women's auxiliaries. Sometimes a woman was made a member just to cook and pick berries, but neither she nor the auxiliaries participated in the truly secret rituals. A few of the tribes had societies whose membership was limited to women. The village tribes of the Upper Missouri had important women's organizations, and among the Pawnees there was a curious association of single women and widows who donned shabby clothing before they tortured prisoners of war. Among the Kiowas, a man starting out on a raid frequently appealed to an organization of forty old women, whom he feasted on his return in gratitude for their prayers. Guilds of skillful tipi cover makers and of expert quill workers existed among the Oglala Sioux.

It may be fairly said, however, that in number, impact, and magnitude the male societies prevailed over the village.

They were called Warrior Societies, and the title itself explains their main purpose. Their function, though, was really a fourfold one: they provided a club atmosphere with the luxury of participation in those mysterious activities limited to the members of a given society, they preserved order in the camp and on organized hunts, they punished offenders against the public welfare, and they cultivated a military spirit among themselves and others—especially young boys—with the ultimate aim of assuring the longevity of the tribe. Often they are

a. Crow Big Dog Society member wearing cap of dried bear guts and sash of hide or trade cloth, and carrying rattle (Lowie reports Crow sash 12 feet long and 5 inches wide). *b,* Crow Hammer Society member. *c,* typical society staff wrapped with otter fur and topped with hawk or owl feathers (Hidatsa). *d,* society buffalo horn rattle. *e,* society leader's wand with eagle claw, beaded handle, and eagle feathers.

referred to simply as police or protective organizations, and in this aspect of life the power of the head or camp chief depended on his cooperation with the societies.

No single society was ever given a monopoly on camp police duty. The headman of the village would call upon one or more of the societies to guard the camp for a stated period, and then they would be replaced by a random selection. The rotation continued until all societies had a turn, and then the cycle would be repeated. Societies were also summoned for specific duties, but even after selection did not act until requested by the headman to do so. Since society membership had nothing to do with family ties or heritage, this, together with the no monopoly principle, tended to blunt any grasping for personal power. Further to prevent the seizure of power and the development of exclusive circles of warriors, retirements and new recruits caused society personnel to change from year to year.

This latter fact, however, did not exclude all vestiges of arrogance. A highly competitive spirit was engendered, and a society which was enjoying a season of prestige because of its brilliant military accomplishments might well assert itself in ways well calculated to make its superiority known. The Peigan Brings Down the Sun told Walter McClintock how his powerful Braves Society expected people of the village to give them whatever they wanted. Failing this, they simply took it. Often they marched through the camp shouting orders. "If people bothered us or got in our way, the bear braves shot at them with arrows." Surely they

Mandan war leader in ermine headdress with split buffalo horns, wearing ancient-style elk shirt (circa 1830), carrying captured crow medicine ring with rock medicine on the ground. Captured was trophies were often used as goads to excite warriors in preparation for a revenge raid.

didn't wound their own people, but the intent was clear. Sometimes the Braves punished women who picked wild berries against their orders by tearing their lodges to pieces! (McClintock, Southwest Museum Leaflet No. 8, pp. 18-30)

Not incidentally, it was the Warrior Societies which fostered the creation of the most marvelous and enthralling of the Plains costumes. And a society dance was an entrancing thing to see. However, with few exceptions the secret and religious aspects of the groups led them to perform for Native American audiences only. Fortunately a few White men were allowed to witness them, and thus were given the privilege of recording their apparel and rituals. George Catlin drew and painted several of the society dances—especially those of the Mandans—and Walter McClintock was able to take some extraordinary photographs of the Blackfoot divisions. Robert Lowie and John Ewers have provided excellent written accounts of Crow and Blackfoot societies, and museums have collected enough society articles that, by adding all of this information together, a rather comprehensive picture of the societies can be drawn today.

There were two types of Warrior Societies, and historians have classified them as age-graded societies and non-graded societies. Simply put, membership in the age-graded societies was determined by the age of the participants. The first or lowest grade consisted of boys approximately fifteen years of age and up who had made a successful vision quest and gone on a first successful raid. The next grade might begin at

Mounted Crow named Shot in the Hand wearing long dog soldier sash and carrying society staff and shield—after 1880 photograph by Lothrop, "The Boy with the U.S. Indians."

age eighteen or so, with the ages for the successive steps in all instances varying with each tribe. Membership of non-graded societies had nothing to do with age. A warrior with noteworthy accomplishments or promise might be invited to join a society regardless of how old he was.

In the age-graded scheme, each warrior passed through all of the societies in turn as he advanced in years. In the non-graded scheme, a warrior usually belonged to a single society for the period of his active warrior life, retiring from all society activities at the average age of forty or so. On rare occasions in both schemes, however, an outstanding warrior might be invited to join more than one society at the same time.

Most society groups were small, numbering from ten to twenty persons, although powerful societies with as many as sixty or more members were known to exist. Usually, the society had a "charmed maximum number" which its founder had received in the vision which gave the society birth. This meant that recruits were invited only at those times when the group had sustained losses through retirements or deaths.

Each society had its own name, and its own tipi or ceremonial lodge which was painted with symbols and colors given to the society founder in his original vision. And it also had its own special medicine bundle. On any given day some of the members gathered in the club lodge to foster their association in the accepted club manner. Each society had its traditional ceremonies and annual festivals, when the awesome medicine bundles were opened, and at such times every member was present.

It should be mentioned that the apparel, etc., of a certain society was respected by all others, and exact duplications were avoided. Somehow the visions never caused the founders to violate the principle.

Society names were both descriptive and captivating. For example, the age graded societies of the Blackfoot were named in grade order as follows: the Doves (or youths); the Mosquitoes (men who went to war); the Braves (or tried warriors); the Brave Dogs; the Kit Foxes; and the Bulls, who were the oldest in origin and held the highest standing. Of these, the first four were most often called upon for police duty.

In 1833 Maximilian set forth a list of the intriguing names of the ten nongraded societies of the Hidatsa tribe: Stone Hammers, Lumpwoods, Crow Indians, Kit Foxes, Little Dogs, Dogs, Half-shaved Head, Black Mouths, Bulls, and Ravens. (Lowie, *The Crow Indians,* p. 173)

It is important to add that while the different tribes often had clubs bearing the same names, the rank of these clubs would usually vary with its tribe. A Kit Fox might be a first-rank society in one tribe and a fourth in another. Also, if a new society of great antiquity was borrowed from another tribe, it was often inserted into the existing scheme at whatever rank the elders of the community felt it deserved. This revised the previous sequence of rank—yet it was not a matter of great consequence since the societies competed at an equal level anyway both at home and on the field of battle.

As the years went by and death, old age, and other circumstances took their toll, some of the societies passed inevitably out of existence.

Sioux dancer wearing crow bustle and roach headdress. The neckpiece of the bustle is on the ground in front of him. *Facing Page*: Back view of dancer in action.

Aged warriors often spoke of once great clubs which had become extinct.

Five tribes—the Mandan, Hidatsa, Blackfoot, Arapaho, and Gros Ventre— employed the age-society system. In this scheme it was customary for young Native American braves to buy the right of their immediate elders to their sets of regalia, dances, and songs, the purchase of which gave them access to the total privileges of the club. In such cases the buyers did not join the sellers as members, but displaced them. The sellers in turn became a cohesive group which jointly bought the emblems and privileges of yet an older group; a process which was repeated at age intervals until the original group of boys had reached the highest and oldest existing grade. When at last they sold their final possessions, they retired from the associational scheme. All males of the five tribes entered the age-graded system and remained within it as age-mates until retirement.

The lively barter involved in these purchases had some delectable features, and these reveal in one more way the Indian's thorough enjoyment of life. For example, the youngest Hidatsa and Mandan groups, called "sons," was always eager to advance, and their "fathers," remembering their own youthful desires, made the most of their advantage, professing the greatest reluctance to give up their beloved dances, badges, and rituals. Hence, the young buyers were obliged to arrive at the sellers' lodge with a great profusion of gifts and a smoking pipe, which would be accepted, but only as a token of the sellers' agreement to discuss the offer. Irrespective of the substance of the discussion, the seniors were sure to declare in the end that the initial offering was insufficient; so the buyers, as they knew they would need to do, held back a reserve supply of gifts, and in addition scurried around to coax more property from their relatives. The older men continued to act as if they were doing their juniors a great favor, until at last a proper tension was reached and began to show itself in the long faces of the sons. Finally the sellers smoked the pipe again, ordering the buyers to bring food to feast their "fathers" for four or more successive evenings. Once more the relatives helped the purchasers to collect the food; then, on the appointed evenings, the sellers received their feasts and began to teach the buyers the songs and dances unique to their society. Continuing the extortion program, the head of the club would exhort the sons to pay generously for the emblems they were to receive. He would also urge them to imitate the example of some of the distinguished fathers as warriors. As the final evening of instructions came to an end, the insignia were turned over to the new members with proper pomp and circumstance, and a public procession and dance followed in which they advertised the fact that they were now the proud representatives of the grade just entered.

Societies which were not graded in any way existed among the Sioux, Assiniboines, Cheyenne, Crows, Pawnees, Arikaras, and the Wind River Shoshones. The Plains Crees had only a single warrior society into which all worthy young men were invited. This club might buy

Omaha two-piece crow bustle made of pheasant feathers (circa 1890).

new dances from another band or nation, and it held two sets of insignia and ceremonial privileges.

The Crow and Cheyenne societies can serve as a typical example of the non-graded type. Membership was voluntary, not dependent on age, and particular societies might hold different levels of rank at different periods of time. The Crow Lumpwoods and Foxes, who were quite similar in insignia and organization, and the Cheyenne Dogs were the most important societies in the tribes during the years 1800 to 1875. While the age system tended to eliminate the status rivalry between societies, wherever non-age-graded clubs ranked as virtual equals, serious competition often set in. Thus the Lumpwoods and the Foxes sought valiantly to outdo each other annually in striking the first blow against an enemy, and the same kind of rivalry existed between many of the Sioux groups.

Every society of either type had its own medicine, or sacred, bundle which contained the objects the founder had been directed to in his initial vision and subsequent visions. The Brave Dog Society bundle of the Piegans contained a war bridle and a whip, and the members carried it to war because of its protective power. It was also used on other important occasions. When not in service it hung from a pole in the society lodge. On another pole hung the society's special rattle, a banner decorated with ermine, an eagle feather warbonnet, and a weasel tailsuit— which was itself looked upon as a medicine bundle. Most societies had their own decorated flags and staffs, which were so well known as to identify the society whenever they were carried.

Each society had its own special songs, which stressed the nature of the club and the ideal of the warlike spirit so necessary to preserve the tribe. Members sang their songs constantly as reminders; in camp, on the trail, when riding into battle, and in ringing unison at the traditional society gatherings. Such songs were considered to have a special power and were to accompany all ritual acts to make the acts effective.

Above all, a society member was expected to be very brave, and only the bravest of all were selected as club officers. Officers were distinguished from other members of the society by their superior regalia, and were deliberately to flout danger. Thus, while the rank-and-file members—or as the Native Americans called them, "lay members"—of the Oglala Sioux Kit Fox organization wore their dance costume of kit fox skin necklaces, a forehead band decorated with kit fox jawbones, and at the back of the head a crown of crow tail feathers and two erect eagle feathers, the officers were distinguished from the rest by their yellow-painted bodies, and four of them who carried special lances revealed by this that they were under a vow to lead in battle and never retreat. Lances such as those just mentioned, straight or curved over at the top, were common society regalia in Plains organizations. (Fletcher, *Teton Sioux Music,* pp. 314-18)

The Crow Foxes and Lumpwoods had two officers, elected for one summer season only, who each carried curved-end otter-skin-wrapped staffs. Two other officers bore long straight staffs with eagle feathers on

Assiniboine Bear Cult member wearing perforated skin shirt with grizzly bear fur pendants tied on his cult staff (after Ewers, *Indian Life on the Upper Missouri*, p. 133).

their smaller end. The straight staff put the staff bearer in a potentially perilous place, for he was required to plant his staff in the ground during a fight. While it was in the ground it represented Crow country. If no fellow society member rode or walked between him and the enemy he was duty-bound to stand by it until either the Crows triumphed or he died; or as the Indians described it, "dropped his robe." Once "ridden between," however, he could relocate the staff in a more favorable location with honor. Staff bearer coups counted double, since their lives were always in special danger while "carrying the stick" in battle. They were self-appointed in a simple ceremony. The head of the society, after asking who would next carry the sticks, passed the pipe. The two men taking the pipe were thereby engaged to carry the sticks for the season. (Lowie, pp. 181-92)

The Crow Big Dog Society was led by a pair of bear-belt wearers. The belt was made of bearskin with the legs and claws still attached. Members painted their bodies with mud and bunched up their hair to resemble a bear's ears. Belt wearers did not hold an enviable position, though, since they had to vow to walk straight up to the enemy in time of danger. They were never to retreat, and were required to rescue imperiled tribesmen.

The bear-belt wearers were followed in rank by two or four sash wearers. The distinctive sash was made of hide or trade cloth, and either hung diagonally over the shoulder by a loop at the end or had a slit to put the wearer's head through. The first style hung down the wearer's

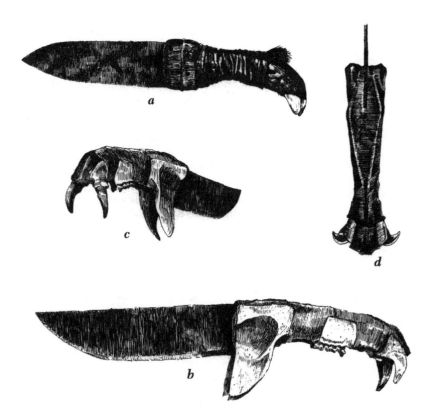

a, Typical ancient Blackfoot Bear Cult knife. The metal blade is double-edged stabber type and the handle is a bear's jawbone. *b,* less typical Blackfoot Bear knife dating from late nineteenth century which shows sculpture quality of knife: single-edged metal blade, jaw handle is covered with sinew. *c,* rear view. *d,* top view.

side, and the second down the middle of his back. The sash was usually over twelve feet in length and was five or so inches wide. It trailed behind the warrior while he was afoot and sometimes reached the ground while he was mounted on a horse. Its length was necessary to give the sash wearer some mobility in war, for he drove his staff through the end of it when he planted the staff in the ground. During a dance, the lay members led the officers around by their sash. Part of the Crow sash wearer's special regalia was a cap covered with dried bear guts. It was painted red and worn because wearing it would impart the animal's strength and ferocity to the warrior. Such caps were often worn into battle, as were selected other items characteristic of the society.

The members of some societies earned the right to wear gorgeous feather dance bustles called "crows." These consisted of a single large bustle belted to the back at the waist, and in some cases of a second and smaller one tied to the back of the neck. These are often a part of the costumes worn by mounted Sioux warriors in old war pictographs, but while they did wear them in parades—and the crow had a split tail for that very reason—they were primarily a dance garment and never worn into battle. They were so splendid that no Native American would risk ruining one and they were not collapsible so as to be easily carried on the trail. Therefore, their main use in pictographs was to identify the wearer. The grandest ones made toward the end of the nineteenth century were constructed of pheasant feathers, but earlier ones were made of golden eagle, hawk, owl, and other feathers. In considering

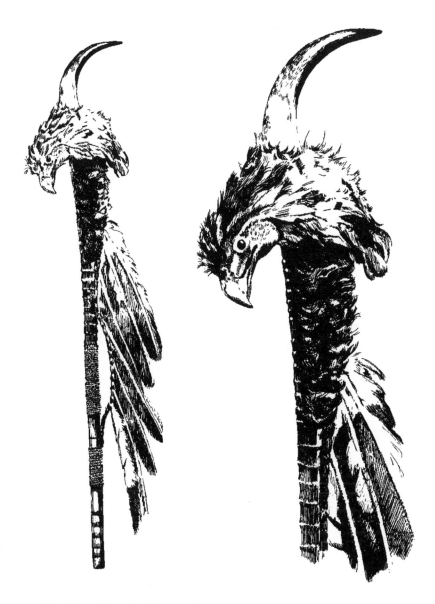

Chief's eagle-head staff with buffalo horn, and eagle feather and strap on handle. Close-up of head at right.

these, one must remember that everything the Native American used for his costume was selected for better reasons than mere decoration. The following description of the Omaha crow bears this out very well:

A man who had attained more than once to honors of the first three grades became entitled to wear a peculiar and elaborate ornament called "the Crow." This was worn at the back, fastened by a belt around the waist; it was made with two long pendants of dressed skin painted red or green, which fell over the legs to the heels. On the skin were fastened rows of eagle feathers arranged to hang freely so as to flutter with the movements of the wearer. An entire eagle skin, with head, beak, and tail, formed the middle ornament; from this rose two arrow shafts tipped with hair dyed red. On the right hip was the tail of a wolf; on the left the entire skin of a crow. This composite decoration illustrated certain ideas that were fundamental to native beliefs, namely: that man is in vital connection with all forms of life; that he is always in touch with the supernatural, and that the life and the acts of the warrior are under the supervision of Thunder as the god of war. This relation was believed to be an individual one and any war honor accorded was the recognition of an individual achievement. Such a bestowal was the outcome of the native method of warfare, for there was no military organization, like an army, in the tribe, and strictly speaking, no commanding officer of a war party; when the battle was on, each man fought for and by himself. A valorous deed was therefore the man's own act and the honor which was accorded the kind of act performed was accredited by Thunder through the representative birds associated with Thunder and contained in the Sacred Pack.

"The Crow" decoration is said to symbolize a battlefield after the conflict is over. The fluttering feathers on the pendants represented the dropping of feathers from the birds fighting over the dead bodies. Sometimes the wearer of "the Crow" added to

Sioux Omaha Dancer. Dance is better known as the Grass Dance because dancers wore braided grass in their belts to symbolize the scalps of their enemies. The dance came from the Omaha tribe and was the most popular social dance of the entire Plains. Many of the dancers carried a wooden whistle with its head carved to look like a crane.

the realism by painting white spots on his back to represent the droppings of birds as they hovered over the bodies of the slain. The two arrow shafts had a double significance; they represented the stark bodies and also the fatal arrows standing in a lifeless enemy. The eagle was associated with war and with the destructive powers of the Thunder and the attendant storms. The wolf and the crow were not only connected with carnage but they had a mythical relation to the office of "soldiers," the designation given to certain men on the annual tribal hunt, who acted as marshals and kept the people and the hunters in order during the surround of the herd. These men were chosen from those who had the right to wear "the Crow" and this regalia was generally worn at that time. It was worn also at certain ceremonial dances.

Omahas, BAE 27th Report, pp. 441-42

The Cheyenne Fox Society member carried a stringless bow and a rawhide rope and pin which was tied at the belt and was called a "dog rope." Fox members were to follow the habits of the fleet and competent fox, who was swift in retreat, but a terror when cornered.

If a Cheyenne Fox member chose, he could make a vow before a battle to drive his pin into the ground and tie himself to it with his dog rope as the enemy closed in. He would then remain there and fight until either the enemy was beaten or he was killed. Others could stand with him and try to save him if they wished to. A warrior who sided a pinned comrad four times gained the eminent right to free a friend in future wars; he could intervene when the warrior was about to be killed, pull the pin, lash him across the back with it, and by so doing cancel the vow.

The Fox (or Dog Men) became one of the leading Cheyenne military societies. Many of its members took the suicide vow each year. It even received a special nickname, and was called "the old men's charm." When the members paraded around the camp before a battle the older men would flank them and sing their praises "as men about to die in the bravest way possible." (Dorsey, *The Cheyenne,* pp. 20-24)

Most young boys formed imitation organizations which were patterned after the warriors' societies, although a few of their groups, such as the Crow Act Like Dogs, had no counterpart in the older men's groups. Dressed only in breechclouts and moccasins, the Act Like Dogs would go outside the camp and smear their bodies with white clay. Then they would sneak to the edge of the village, and at a given signal, scatter and run through the lodges, barking and growling like dogs while they wildly snatched at choice pieces of meat which had been hung to dry. The villagers joined in the game with great enthusiasm. The old men fell back in supposed fear, and the women cried out in mock alarm, running after the "dogs" with sticks and, in a playful manner, harassing them. Sometimes the women threw pieces of meat at them as they would at their own dogs. When each youth had collected enough meat, the group went back to the woods, washed in a nearby creek or spring, cooked the meat at a campfire, had a sumptuous feast, and animatedly discussed their happy adventure. (Linderman, *Plenty Coups,* pp. 20-22)

A Crow society, called the Hammers, was exclusively for boys about sixteen years of age. Usually, little was required of them, but in serious emergencies the same bravery was expected of them as of the other

Blackfeet Elk Medicine Pipe Dance.

society members. Their emblem was a small, elongated wooden (or stone) hammerhead. It was mounted on a wooden shaft over eight feet in length. Some of these were painted with white clay and decorated with a long, erect feather at the top, while at three distinct points along the pole were two other feathers and a bunch of shorter ones. Other models were adorned with yellow and red or yellow and blue paint, put on in stripes corresponding to the body colors of their owners. (Lowie, pp. 202-6)

Mystic animal cults were numerous among the tribes of the Great Plains. Each of these entrancing groups was composed of individuals who believed they had obtained supernatural power from the same animal or bird through a dream or vision. Like the societies, they evolved distinctive ritual and ceremonial regalia associated with the animal from which the cult's power was derived.

The Bear Cult was a prime example. It was composed of a small number of men in nearly every tribe who believed they had obtained a supernatural bear power through dreams. They painted bear symbols on their tipis and shields. When a cult member died, his power went away to the great hunting ground with him. It could not be transferred to another person.

This cult performed several major functions: It conducted ceremonies in honor of the bear, it held bear feasts and ceremonial bear hunts. It participated aggressively in war expeditions, and it doctored the sick.

When participating in any of these activities, the Assiniboine Bear Cult member shaved the middle of his head and rolled some of the remaining hair at each side into a ball resembling a bear's ear. He painted his entire face red, and then made vertical bear claw marks on each side of it by scraping away some of the paint with his fingernails. After this he painted a black circle around each eye and around his mouth. He wore a bear claw necklace over a yellow-painted skin shirt, which was perforated all over in a unique way with round holes, and further decorated with cut fringes along the bottom edge and the sleeve ends. A small, rectangular flap of skin was cut in the shirt at the center of the wearer's chest, and the flap hung down the front. (Ewers, *Indian Life on the Upper Missouri*, p. 133)

The Bear member also carried a glorious kind of knife. It had a broad, flat, single- or double-edged metal blade whose handle was made from a bear's jawbone. It was a piece of graceful sculpture without fault. The Blackfoot bear knife is a superb example of this ancient art.

When a member of the Bear Cult went into action against the enemy he always wore his distinctive bear outfit, and since bears were noted for their ferocious attacks, a charging cult member made a grunting noise like a bear and made every effort to be as much a bear as possible!

Every warrior in every tribe had a bird or animal patron of one species or another. Each man sought to duplicate the attributes of his patrons when engaged in a war. In the Native American's mind a man did not fight another warrior, but rather a bear, a buffalo, an eagle, an ermine, or the like. And because each warrior wore some sign or a part

Gros Ventre Fly Society Dance.

of his society regalia into battle, if it was plain enough to be seen an enemy could size up what sort of an animal or bird he was fighting. He then adjusted his attack accordingly. Played out to its fullest extent the habit added some wonderful facets to the Plains encounters.

A delightful trait designed to break the potential austerity of an overdone traditional life was provided by societies called "contraries," which were found in each tribe. Members of these were obliged to say the opposite of what they meant and to do the opposite of whatever was demanded of them. Generally, they behaved in a way contrary to common sense. If one said "go," he really meant "come." Oglala Sioux contrary society members were seen plunging their arms into very hot water, and then splashing it over each other, complaining all the while that it was freezing cold.

When one pauses to assess the ultimate value of the societies in the social scheme of the Plains, he finds that the Native Americans have already done it for him. The venerable Crow chief Plenty Coups revealed how captivating and how effective societies were in the perpetuation of a Crow boy's individual responsibility to the tribe as a whole when he said:

> That night the secret societies held meetings, the Foxes, the Warclubs, the Big-dogs, the Muddy-hands, the Fighting-bulls, and others. Bright fires blazed and crackled among the pines, and drums were going all night long. I wished with all my heart that I might belong to one of these secret societies. I thought most of the Foxes, and I looked with longing eyes at their firelit

lodge, where men spoke of things I could not know. But I was yet only a boy.

Linderman, p. 53

It has been seen that Plains Indian social life was carried out at four levels: the family, the community (or village), the tribe, and the society. In each of the last three levels social life expressed itself more in songs and dancing than in all other types of social activities put together.

In fact, it is impossible to refer to the Plains Indians of old without speaking of songs and dancing, for these played a continual and vital part in their lifescheme. They had dances for almost every occasion. These were seldom indulged in for exercise and amusement. Usually they were performed as integral parts or expressions of the more serious things in life. More narrowly, the dances were an activity intended to heighten and sharpen every worthwhile thought and emotion.

The Native American dancer saw, heard, and felt the story he was trying to portray with a peculiar intensity, and because of this he usually enacted it so well that it was not difficult for his informed and sympathetic audience to catch the meaning of his every motion. It has often been said that in some dances the degree of acting was so intense that whole scenes of history came to life, and in the case of animal dances the dancers seemed to become the beings they were impersonating.

Many of the dances were religious ceremonials, whose intent was to gain wisdom from or give thanks to the supernatural powers. Some of the dances were associated with warfare, and these were held before a

Bear Dance, Arikara Medicine Ceremony.

war party started out as well as on its victorious return. There were comic, healing, peace, victory, mourning, and hunting dances, dances of a purely social type, and in the more stationary villages of the Mandans and Pawnees, planting and harvest dances. Some dances were performed exclusively by men, and some solely by women. In other instances men and women danced together. Some dances were held in which anyone might take part, and others were limited to a single dancer selected for the occasion. Many dances, as was true in the case of the society songs, were private property, and could only be performed by their rightful owners. Each of the Plains Indian societies had dances that centered in the themes of mystery and war. Some dances to be used while curing the sick were owned by individual holy men, and some by societies of medicine men. However, it should also be pointed out that every ritual was not a dance, and the word "dance" has often been wrongly applied by White men to some of the great Native American rituals in which dancing actually played but a small part. This is especially true of what are commonly referred to as the Calumet, Ghost, and Sun Dances.

All Native American dances followed traditional forms. Some of the dance steps were simple, but others were complicated and quite difficult to learn. And the male style differed from the female. When men danced the heel and ball of each foot in turn was lifted and brought down with considerable force, so as to produce a thudding sound. The changes of their position were slow, but the shifts in attitude were rapid and sometimes violent. Women employed the shuffle, the glide, the hop, and the

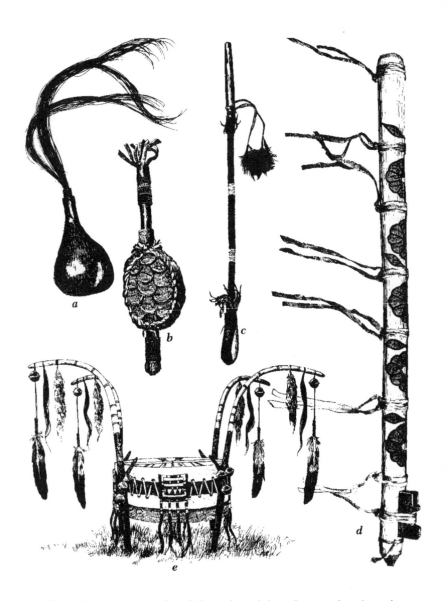

Musical instruments. *a*, deer hide rattle with horsehair pendant. *b*, turtle shell rattle. *c*, drum beater with beaded handle. *d*, wooden flute with rawhide fringes (34 inches long). *e*, four-man drum.

leap. Usually, dancers moved in a clockwise circle direction, "with the sun." When dancing with the men, women were usually placed in an inside circle.

Every song, prayer, and dance connected with a ceremony was to be performed according to its traditional form, for it was believed that serious misfortune would come to the performers immediately upon the heels of any deliberate failure to give a strictly accurate performance. Informers report that if anything went wrong, the ceremony must either begin again or else be abandoned, although while that seems to rule out enjoyment, Native Americans often had a good laugh after a ceremony had ended during which there had been a humorous mistake. The value of adherence to traditional forms can easily be seen. For example, in the dances where personal experiences were portrayed the dancer was allowed some freedom of invention, yet even here the performer was compelled to parallel conventional forms or else his story would not be understood by his audience, which interpreted the dance by making comparisons with tradition. The need to perform the dances along traditional lines did not, however, interfere with the development of new dances or prevent the spread of a certain dance from one tribe to another. Nor did it prevent real happiness in dancing, for the Plains Indian appreciated, and did not regret, his place in a long line of heirs.

In order to maintain their distinctiveness, the different tribes usually varied their ways of performing dances bearing the same name. The Crows would not do a Bear Dance in exactly the same way as the Hidatsas.

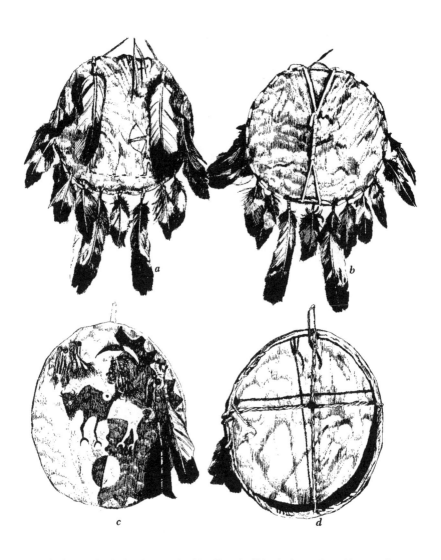

Lightweight hide dance shields: *Top,* buffalo hide with golden eagle feathers—*a,* front; *b,* back. *Bottom,* elk hide with metal bell and quill strip thumpers, very old style on wooden hoop frame—*c,* front; *d,* back. Rough diameter of both shields, 18 inches. Hides used for dance shields were much thinner than those of war shields.

Sioux victory dancer carrying hide-wrapped sacred sage and also a victory wreath, and wearing crow bustle (circa 1876).

Society dances were also shaped until they had established a distinct identification within each tribe. Some dances originated with each tribe, and were indigenous. Others were borrowed by one tribe from another.

The Crow Bear Song Dance and the Singing of the Cooked Meat—a semi-annual occasion for rock-medicine owners to open their sacred bundles—were indigenous. Other Crow dances, like the Medicine Pipe Ritual and the Horse Dance, were the products of visits with other tribes, usually their Hidatsa kinsmen. The Crow Bear Song Dance performers were known by their ability to produce from their mouths parts of a creature or object which had "miraculously" entered their stomachs during a fast. Among those things revealed were such unappetizing objects as elk chips, white clay, black dirt, owl feathers, ground moss, snails, eggs, feathers from an eagle's tail, and, commonly, parts of the bodies of bears and jackrabbits. People owning renowned horses would exhibit horse tails; and those who had proven they could doctor wounds, buffalo tails. Usually the Bear Dance was held in the fall, when the ripe berries "caused the bears to dance in the mountains."

Music for the dances would be furnished by the singing of the dancers and the playing of the instruments they carried, or else by a separate chorus and orchestra. Sometimes the dancers and orchestra combined their talents. If a chorus was used the singers either gathered around the drum, stood or sat as a group to one side, or else stood in the center of the circle of dancers. There were moments in some dances when the orchestra would cease playing while the dancers provided their own

Sioux Indian women. Girl at left wears dentalium beaded dress and hair-pipe bone necklace. Mother at bottom right has hair cut short in mourning for deceased husband.

accompaniment, after which the process was reversed or the two would combine. Drums, flutes, whistles, and rattles were the principal instruments used by orchestras and dancers to accompany the singing. Time was generally marked by the drum.

While Whites were usually gripped by the pulsating drumbeat which accompanied Native American dancing and singing, the first reaction to their songs was often a disagreeable one. To avoid this one had to learn that the Native American's mind was on the force behind the songs. He did not only sing and listen to a song, he also lived it; it was a means of accomplishing transformations within himself so that he could bring his person into accord with the Spirit, with the universe, and with his fellow man.

The throbbing of the drum, which to him was the heartbeat of the world, combined with his words and pulled his thoughts into a tangible form he could deal with. In practice, the seemingly unmelodious sounds were transformed into a series of related phrases which spoke infinite meanings to his mind and heart. Thus it is easy to see why the Plains Indian developed a song for every moment of his life, and why all of these made deep and abiding contributions to his happiness.

Traditional and ceremonial songs, like dances, were considered to be the property of the tribal leaders or of an individual, depending upon which received them first, and they must be bought, traded, or given as a gift before they could be used by anyone else. Native Americans had an amazing facility for memorizing the songs, and some could sing hundreds of verses without a mistake. Fortunately, and perhaps not accidentally, most songs were very short; as such, a stanza or two would be repeated over and over again. Bearing the main intent in mind, one can appreciate that the repetition only increased the ultimate value received.

Indeed, simplicity was the keynote for Native American songs and no attempt was made to duplicate the White man's often complicated verbiage.

Typical Plains Indian songs were as follows:

The Fox
I am; something
difficult
I seek

Owls
were hooting
in the passing of the night
owls
were hooting

This honored one,
this honored one,
horses
I donated

Sacred
he made for me
sacred
he made for me
a blacktail deer

The reflective pipe smoker meditating upon how the pipe connected him with God (after Olaf Seltzer). *Right:* Sioux pipe smoker preparing to "speak straight" by smoking the straight pipe.

sacred
he made for me
those
you had seen

In considering their brevity, several important points besides those already mentioned should be borne in mind. First, they could be brief because the circumstances of their composition and rendition would be well known to all the members of the band. It would not be necessary to include the more intimate details. Second, the songs served to emphasize the main point of a story, and were kept simple so the point would be easily understood and remembered by an audience. Third, traditional phrases were used, and as such evoked traditional responses from the audience. The phrases, then, served to promote a familiar atmosphere for each song. Fourth, the very abstraction of the brief statements provided an aura of mystery, and like an incomplete painting, a Plains song tended to draw the listener into the singer's life experience of the moment. Fifth, the words, phrases, and stanzas were repeated many times. In rituals, the stanzas were usually repeated in sets of fours or sevens, both of which were considered to be sacred numbers. The aim was to rhyme thoughts, not sounds, and as such to achieve a familiarity which brought a sense of comfort and security to both the singer and his audience.

There was no part singing or harmonizing, for harmonizing would have interfered with the basic purpose. Instead, each Native American sang his song with maximum force, following impulses rather than a melody rule book. Often the measure of the drumbeat differed from that of the song, for the drum controlled the body movements while the song was geared to the soul. In a way, this tended to draw the entire person into the dancing activity. Martin Luther once remarked upon the infinite wisdom of God, who in the sacraments gave us a material element that the body could experience, and in the Word, a spiritual element that could be absorbed by the soul. The idea, as Luther saw it, was that the activity of the ritual *involved the total man*. Apparently the Great Mystery was able to communicate such comprehensive under-standings to the Native Americans as well, for they came to the same concept, and put it to the best of uses.

Personal Qualities

Once the true nature or life-way of the ancient Plains Indians becomes clear, several profound opportunities present themselves. First, there is the distinct possibility that by adopting some parts of the Native American life-way we can at last recapture a portion of that superb freedom, adventure, and happiness which characterized the Plains dweller of 1750 to 1875. Second, we can now share in certain valuable religious truths of the Native Americans which have been kept secret or were overlooked. Third, the charity and hospitality of the Plains Indians could easily offer itself as an ideal model for the world. Fourth, since they were a creative and inventive people of such a unique kind, that aspect of their life can now be added to the many abilities already possessed in creative areas.

The reason these opportunities have not presented themselves until now is that non-Native Americans have been merely spectators concerning the Native Americans, and so have missed the proverbial forest because of preoccupation with the trees. Nearly everything about the Native American has been considered save his greatest aspect, his superb process of mental preparation for life, and how that process affected and

Part of a mounted war party carrying feathered lances and coup sticks.

improved everything he did. By it, he learned to flow, not fight, with God and nature, and the rest of mankind could profit greatly by being, for a while at least, his student instead of his teacher.

Comparing them to the White race, early writers who had but scanty or hearsay knowledge of the Native Americans usually described them as a limited or "savage" people. Yet the comparison was a decidedly unfair one, for the Native American's life and mind was not geared to function like those of the average man of the industrial world. He was shaped by his natural religion, by his elders, and by his primitive and wild surroundings. Associating on the most intimate basis with extreme natural conditions and with only the people of his own race, his standard of wisdom and learning became that of nature, and of the wise men of his tribe who had earned their positions as teachers through practical experience.

Thus he inevitably came to act as nature did and to think as the elders thought. His reasoning processes remained much the same as those of the generations before him. Slight advances in culture were brought about from time to time by new influences, such as the horse and trade with the Whites, but except for the expansion and intensification of craftworks, the general cultural change in all parts of the Plains from 1750 to 1875 was slight, and happened at a leisurely pace. It is important, in saying this, to recognize that by "culture" I mean the Native American's life-way, and not the externals of existence. Insofar as the life-way is concerned, new influences made little difference in the Native American's

At left, northern Plains style of eagle-wing fan with painted hide handle. At right, southern Plains style of fan where tail feathers make fan and the eagle body and head are attached to the fan handle.

developmental process. Time in particular was the least of his concerns, and he never thought to invent a gadget to measure it or to speed up the manufacturing process. Clocks are only needed by those who endorse the idea of scheduled lives or who believe that true productivity is only determined by inventories taken at the end of a day.

As a rule, the Native American remained without training in most matters having to do with what others call "civilized life." Indeed, moving in the opposite direction, he became a partner of natural existence as it was. And, in respect to things with which he became familiar, he developed abilities sufficient to astonish the Whites who came as the first visitors to his country.

Like the wild bird and beast, like the white clouds and the straight green trees, like the eternal rocks and the crystal streams, the Native American was a part of nature. He became so because he studied the whole of it until little escaped his mind or eye, and then he sought to move with it in a rare kind of conformity. Ultimately, what he received was a special kind of inner peace. It is true that he was wholly unable to reason scientifically, because his directions did not lead him to the kind of information upon which such reasoning might be based. Yet considering the total circumstances, the human product and what he produced are all the more remarkable. And in the end, one is almost forced to wonder whether the Plains life-way is not in many ways preferable to that of the non-Native American.

It is essential to pause here and to summarize the life-way characteristics which resulted from the leisurely evolution of the Plains culture, for without this it is utterly impossible to know what the Plains people were really like, and without this there can be no true understanding of why they so enthusiastically embraced the customs which characterized their day.

Among the members of a given tribe, honesty was an absolute, and lying was sure to bring the direst consequences. The straight stem of the pipe a man smoked represented the need to speak straightly (or truthfully). In matters concerning those things in which he had no positive knowledge, he was exceedingly careful to qualify his statements, so that it never might be said of him that "he had two tongues." Theft was virtually unknown in a Native American village and people could leave their goods unattended without fear. A lost piece of property was immediately delivered to the camp crier, who proclaimed the news of its discovery throughout the camp, so that the owner of the lost article might recover it. However, since it fitted his idea of proper defense, a Native American did not hesitate to take all the property he could from an enemy. Even then the usual loot was horses, and an enemy's village was seldom disturbed or ravaged.

There was universal hospitality and charity within the tribe. Food was always shared. Those who did the actual procuring of an animal, such as a buffalo, might take some small special advantage, but that was all. Except in times of great scarcity, food could be had from a successful hunting party for the asking. So long as there was any food remaining in the lodge, every visitor received his share without the slightest hesitation. Childhood friendships were likely to last throughout the lifetimes of the persons involved. In battle and in cases of special need, friends would often give their lives for each other. Tom Newcomb, a scout for General Miles in the early seventies, and who later lived with the Sioux, stated that he never saw more kindness, charity, and brotherhood anywhere than he did among the Sioux. (Seton, *The Gospel of the Redman*, pp. 2-3)

Respect for parents and for the rights of others and self-control were natural outgrowths of the interdependent Native American community. Serious family or camp quarrels were extremely rare. In all matters of consequence children obeyed their parents and the camp leaders or police societies. It is said that once quarrels did occur, the parties to them were likely to be difficult to control. Each participant would behave as unreasonably as a child, seeing only from his own point of view, and acknowledging no justification on the part of the other. Most serious arguments resulted in the destruction of property, and only rarely in a killing. In such instances the killer might himself be killed by a police society, or he would be cast out of the village. The very least he would suffer would be a total loss of influence and social ostracism. Even a chief or principal man who killed a member of his tribe in self-defense would lose his position of influence and be avoided forever by all the members of the tribe.

People who imagine the Plains Indians to be savages would not

Shoshone warrior and his wife in dignified splendor on fully outfitted horses.

expect to find etiquette in common practice, yet their forms of it would do credit to any nation.

There were many wisdom sayings which were addressed to the young—some of which included admonitions about eating. These had nothing to do with the use of utensils, but more importantly with promoting respect and concern for elders. For example, a boy would be told he should not eat a certain soft part of the buffalo, else his legs would become soft. But the real meaning of the admonition was that he should have the courtesy to leave the tender parts for the aged, who could not chew as well as he. (Omahas, BAE 27th Report, p. 331)

The warmest space in a lodge, the one directly in back of the fire, was reserved for guests. It was the place of honor, and robes were spread there to make the visitors welcome.

A Native American never passed between the fire and another individual unless an apology was first made for cutting him momentarily off from its warmth. The same was true of passing between people who were engaged in conversation.

When a guest came he took his seat quietly and remained so for some time. No one addressed him until he had time to "catch his breath," which really meant time to avoid having any matter hastily introduced. The use of the pipe aided further in such deliberateness. Departures from a tipi after a discussion were made without ceremony. After all, the matter was finished. Why belabor it?

The Indians tell about a courtesy which was practiced between married persons and their in-laws. Direct address was avoided, and an intermediary passed information back and forth between the two. However, the rule was not inflexible, and stories are told about son-in-laws who became close companions of their father-in-laws. (McClintock, *Old North Trail,* p. 334)

Now that the practice has ceased, many have speculated about the purpose of the custom, for it appears awkward at best. Some old Omaha men who were questioned about it thought it was done to show respect for elders. But there are excellent reasons beyond that. In the first place, it avoided direct confrontation over the differing opinions about life that commonly occur between newlyweds and in-laws, and in the second—assuming that the premise about their learning from the same God approximately what the Christian would is a correct one—it would have something to do with a man's "leaving his father and mother and cleaving to his wife," so that the two could live as an unimpeded "one flesh." A person can be neither a good husband nor wife until the umbilical ties with mother and father have been severed.

Etiquette also required that a person's name should not be mentioned in his presence. This practice was intended to deepen the relationship between people—strange as this may at first seem. Others were addressed as father, mother, friend, brother, etc. These were terms of relationships which express a love that is not conveyed when the personal name is used. The Native Americans felt that any impersonal stranger could use a name. In the same way a man of standing would be called "aged man," which granted him the status of wisdom, and which tended to bring forth a profound response.

Politeness forbade a person to ask a stranger's name or even what business had brought him into the community. These awaited the development of events. Now and then an emissary from another tribe came and went without anyone's having learned his name.

Cleanliness was a norm of Plains life, and irrespective of the problems of the elements and constant travel, it was practiced to a commendable degree. Alexander Henry II, a trader during the early 1800s, stated that the Sioux, the Crows, the Cheyenne, and the Mandans had the custom of washing morning and evening. (Henry, *Journal,* Vol. I, p. 325) George Catlin reinforced this, pointing out that while there were many exceptions, the Plains people as a rule observed decency, cleanliness, and elegance of dress. "There are few people, perhaps, who take more pains to keep their persons neat and cleanly, than they do." (Catlin, *North American Indians,* Vol. I, p. 96, Vol. II, p. 233) The stationary village tribes, who had the advantage of nearby rivers, bathed every day in summer and winter. In addition to all of this, the sweat lodge was in common use by young and old alike.

Physical health received a high priority on the Plains, since it was a requisite for survival. The Native Americans followed a demanding system of physical training, and the elders often advised the young to condition themselves properly for the rigors of the mature years ahead. Indulgences, in particular, were curbed. Young men were forced to exercise, and advised not to smoke. Fasting was a regular practice, as was long-distance running and winter swimming. In 1882 a young Cree carrying dispatches ran 125 miles in twenty-five hours, and the feat was so common that it received no comment among the Native Americans. (Seton, p. 47) The health of the Plains people was so good that prior to contact with the Whites no plague-type infectious diseases or mental disorders were known to them.

Responsibility and loyalty were common traits in a Native American community. Every boy was continually nurtured by the admonition that he must become a brave protector of his country and his tribe, and a dependable friend. Here an incredible wrong should be put right. Many authors have stated that Native American men went to war for personal gain and glory; that it gave them wealth and an opportunity to be adored. In short, it was done for vanity's sake alone! But the Native American accounts do not support this contention in any way. Horse raids and warfare were defensive activities designed to keep the enemy off balance and to impair his economic base—so that he could not make massive war. The adulation which followed success in these things was simply a just reward for meeting one's responsibilities in protecting the tribe. Jonathon Carver, commenting upon his visits with the Native Americans, said:

> The honour of their tribe, and the welfare of their nation is the first and most predominant emotion of their hearts; and from hence proceed in a great measure all their virtues and

their vices. Actuated by this, they brave every danger, endure the most exquisite torments, and expire triumphing in their fortitude, not as a personal qualification, but as a national characteristic.

Carver, Travels, p. 271

Pride was one of the most important of the Native American's qualities, for he was proud to be a Native American, and in particular a member of "his" tribe. Moreover, he gladly took his place of responsibility in a continuing line of heirs. History was a vital thing to him. He also placed great store in achievement and its rewards. Few of his tasks were done carelessly; the greater percentage by far were executed with thoroughness, thoughtfulness, and attention to detail.

Joy was a word that belonged to the Native Americans. Life was rich, and the Native Americans were only stoical and sullen in the presence of Whites during the war and reservation period. They were really a *happy,* delightful people, so ready to laugh at an amusing incident or clever joke that they reminded the early White visitors of children at play.

A quote from Colonel Dodge puts this truth very well:

> In his manner and bearing, the Indian is habitually grave and dignified, and in the presence of strangers he is reserved and silent.
> The general impression is that the Indian is a stoic. Nothing can be further from the truth. Stoicism is a "put on." In his own camp, away from strangers, the Indian is a noisy, jolly, rollicking, mischief-loving braggadocio, brimful of practical jokes and rough

fun of any kind, making the welkin ring with his laughter, and rousing the midnight echoes by song and dance, whoops and yells.

He will talk himself wild with excitement, vaunting his exploits in love, war, or the chase, and will commit all sorts of extravagances while telling or listening to an exciting story. In their everyday life Indians are vivacious, chatty, fond of telling and hearing stories. Their nights are spent in song and dance, and for the number of persons engaged, a permanent (safe) Indian camp is at night the noisiest place that can be found.

Dodge, p. 58

Wisdom of a special type was also to be found on the Plains. Joseph Epes Brown, in his book entitled *The Sacred Pipe,* tells how he came after many years of study to believe there was a lofty wisdom among the central Native American people. (Brown, *The Sacred Pipe,* Preface, pp. 9–10) This led him to record and edit the sacred knowledge of the Sioux spiritualist Black Elk, who could neither read nor speak English, and therefore had never read the Bible. Here he found ample evidence to support the fact that the old Native American holy men possessed qualities and degrees of spirituality rarely found in the world today—"for want of which the world is becoming impoverished, in spite of its material wealth." The following paraphrases of the wise teachings of several tribes will in themselves show that what he says was undeniably true.

Any man who is attached to the senses and to the things of this world is one who lives in ignorance and is being consumed by the snakes which represent his own passions.

Our Father has made his will known to us here on this earth, and we must always do that which he wishes if we want to walk the sacred path.

There can never be peace between nations until there is first known that true peace which is within the souls of men. This comes when men realize their oneness with the universe and all its Powers, and when they know that the Great Spirit is at its center, that all things are his works, and that this center is really everywhere, it is within each of us. He watches over and sustains all life. His breath gives life; it is from him and to him that all generations come and go.

Every step we take upon mother earth should be done in a sacred manner; each step should be as a prayer. The power of a pure and good soul is planted as a seed, and will grow in man's heart as he walks in a holy manner. The Spirit is anxious to aid all who seek him with a pure heart.

We are two-legged as the birds are because the birds leave the world with their wings, and we one day leave it in the spirit. This is one of the things we learn from the holy birds.

The breath of the Spirit is seen in the corn, since when the wind blows, the pollen falls from the tassel onto the silk surface surrounding the ear, through which the fruit becomes mature and fertile.

We should all remember how merciful God is in providing for our wants, and in the same manner provide them for children, especially those who are without parents.

The old men tell us that everything they see changes a little during a man's natural lifetime, and that when change comes to any created thing it must accept it, that it cannot fight, but must change.

Our people were wise. They never neglected the young or failed to keep before them deeds done by illustrious men of the tribe. Our teachers were willing and thorough. All were quick to praise excellence without speaking a word that might break the spirit of a boy who might be less capable than others. The boy who failed at any lesson only received more lessons and care, until he was as far as he could go.

A man should rely on his own resources; the one who trains himself is ready for any emergency.

The youth who thinks first of himself and forgets the old will never prosper, nothing will go straight for him.

A man who is not industrious will always have to borrow from others, and will never have things of his own. He will be envious and tempted to steal. He will be unhappy. The energetic man is happy and pleasant to speak with; he is remembered and visited on his deathbed. But no one mourns for the lazy man.

A thrifty woman has a good tipi; all her tools are the best, so is her clothing.